Life of Light

Let your light flow and miracles will follow

Neti

BookLeaf Publishing

India | USA | UK

Illustrations by ____

Presentation by *BookLeaf Publishing*

Web: www.bookleafpub.com

E-mail: info@bookleafpub.com

ISBN: 9789358363821

First edition 2021

*To the little, now grown-up girls
and boys, who forgot their hearts.
To those who forgot to smile.
To those who forgot to say no. To
those who forgot to say yes.
To me, who would rather die than
share my poems with another
soul.
We are. Here. Alive. Connected.
Keep building!*

Acknowledgements

Thank you to all the humans who served as my mirror with the hardest lessons. I would not have faced myself without you. I am grateful for what has passed.

Thank you even more to my soul supporters in the present, for without you I might have lost it... you know who you are!

And thank you to a special Turtle, for the love, support and laughter!

Preface

This book contains a slice of Universe -
the closer you look, the more elusive it
becomes.

Close your eyes and take a bite! Allow it
in your heart.

And remember: words are spells, that is
why we call it *spelling*…!

1. The beginning

A fountain,

of marble, yet alive

with a bench on its side

made of stone, yet a home

a home that was mine

two millennia ago

and you, sitting there

right beside me

long forgotten yet alive in my heart

my dear sister

the iris of my eye

precious, beautiful, protecting

how could have I forgotten you?

my heart remembers you

your curly hairs

your deep green eyes

your presence, nurturing and loving

your motherly embrace

that day you came to me

at long last

that day

my heart unleashed

a river, with no beginning and no end

overwhelming love

pouring in me

in waves

my being filled with sweetness

with the boundless love

beyond all time

within all space

you always were there

weren't you?

always by my side

embracing me with presence

loving me in silent stride

waiting

being

patiently

for me to see

what was right there

always there

in me

I am!

and you are, too

you guide my steps

you give me choice

thank you, Filo!

goddess of my heart

and yet the sweetest sister

anyone could ever have

thank you

for your sweet everless embrace

thank you

for catching me before I fall

thank you

for being

beyond existence

all I know

is that in the boundless expense

there's beauty, love, and wisdom

waiting

for me to reach out

and ask.

for me... to be

for all of us.

2. Now

They are endless

an everlasting

evergiving

abundance

each moment

the eternal now

offers us the beauty

of a gemstone

adorning our souls

gifting us a countless

stream

of joy, experiences, colour

the tragedy of life is

we overlook

each now

we overlook

life

3. **And you?**

When I am on a plane

flying

on a hill

climbing

after a cold

healing

anywhere, anyhow, anywho

comes a moment

I hear my

ears

pop

in that moment

I clearly remember

oh yes, that is how

hearing feels

I didn't even notice

it was gone

it hurts a little

or a little more

it feels a little off

and yet, oh, the beauty of the sounds!

now imagine

that pop

and suddenly

remembering

to see

the crispness of air

to hear

the exquisite song of nature

to know

that which cannot be said

a pop in human nature

an inner pop

and in an instant

back to who I was

always

and always will be

and you

4. Human

Silence

in my bones

heaviness

in my mind

numbness

in my body

and yet

I am here, watching

the movie of

my life

fully involved

and yet

a bystander

an eternal being

driving through

my human existence

while human is overlooking

the obvious

the uniqueness

of raindrops

the silence

of the moon

the taste

of turmeric tea

I'm here, too

savoring it

being

5. Moonlight

I have seen a thousand lives

each unique

each a journey

in each I loved, hated, died

and learned

so I'm here, now

looking at the crescent

she remains unchanged

yet, phases in and out

just like I did

my moon

you and I

have a secret

still untold

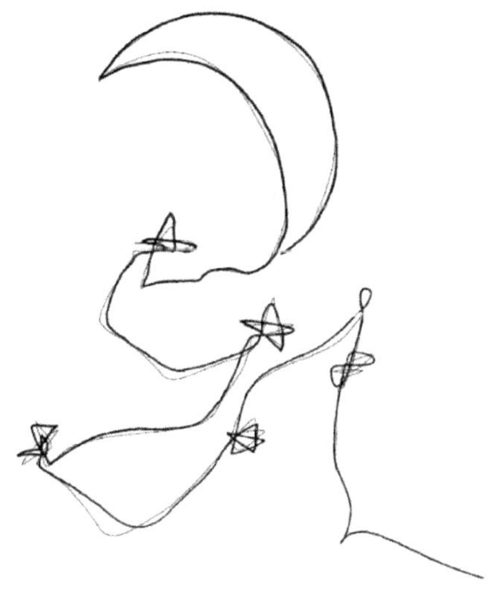

6. Gift

There is a world

out there

in the boundless expanse

full of flowers

colour

freshness

full of beauty

streams

abundance

full of life

warmth

and sound

a home

and it is this one

it was a gift for us!

ours for the taking, ours for the making

it is a gift today

a gift created out of love

and the gift is also us

the here in the now

and it is ours to cherish

or to divide

and it is ours to marvel

or to destroy

and it is ours to embrace in fulness

or to hate and fear

as a perfect gift, given from the heart to

us

we are granted the ultimate permission

and with it comes free will

to decide

what it is that we do

with it

in it

with ourselves

for we are also part of it

we were given all the tools to

feel it, taste it, see it, smell it, hear it

the laughter, love, the joy

the sights and sounds of heaven

the tastes and aromas too

the pleasantness of being here, now

and we know all this, in our hearts

what are we doing?

7. Moments

We were gifted

the endless space of time

between one second

and the next

just like the eternity

hiding

between the zero and the one

we have ourselves decided

to overlook that

priceless gift

of the wonder that

the present moment

offers

by looking forward

to a better future

and regretting

our (invented) past

8. Silence

Sometimes I rest

quietly

under the blanket of existence

and hear its song

it sings a quiet tune

a melody beyond my ears

its song about birth and death

it sings of being

of the wholeness.

it hugs us

close to our hearts

it gives us breath

it is a lullaby

to keep us awake

yet instead,

we sleep

deaf to its beauty

blind to its song

numb to its loving

honey,

what holds you on the edge?

you are pure heart

you are made of living wholeness

take a break

look around

hear the song

of Life

9. I

I looked in the mirror
saw her look back at me
heard her tell me

you are a force of nature

a gentle one
like water
liquid love
crystal light

gentle yet powerful

I am here to stay
I never truly left
I needed her

so you can hear me

so you can see me

yet I am much more

beyond all you can see

I am
magic
magnetism
intuition
powerful
free
beautiful
love
eternal
limitless
a natural woman

I am

a force of nature

an innate light

come claim me

10. The temple

I climbed a mountain

made of the colours of the

rainbow

red

orange

yellow

green

blue

purple

and right there at the top

was bright

bright white light

showering a temple

humbly, I stepped in

humbly, yet with power

as soon as those gates

opened up before my being

I could feel all the past

lifted off my shoulders

I was light

I was as a feather

free

finally myself

the long-forgotten self

of millennia ago

who keeps coming back

to learn, to lead, to be

here I am

once again

bathing in the temple candlelight

welcoming the aroma of completeness

into the deepest corners of my being

breathing life

bowing to the Force of Nature

that I am

a ray of light

a wise ray

facing the Creator

refracted

into a rainbow

into me

the temple vanished

only I and her remained

Existence

we shall meet again.

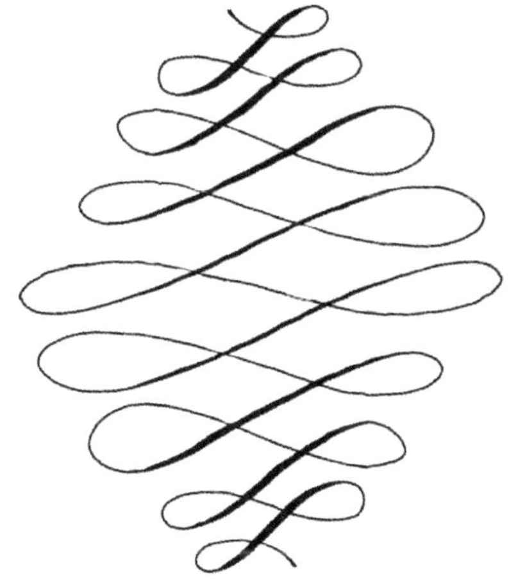

11. Reflection

She stares back at me

I see her eyes

her hair, features, smile

she looks back at me

as if smiling

greeting me

and I am here

gazing back into her hazel eyes

remembering all the other faces

that were had before

a little curly boy

and an emerald-eyed goddess

all the seen and the unseen

all the wins, all the loses

lives fully lived

lives full of joy and sorrow

here she is again

new face, new clothes, new era

learning yet again

to take her first steps into the world

a life young

yet wise

wisdom forever shining through her

spirit

hello there

remember me?

I always will look after you

I will be with you

until you walk this planet

I will never let you down

I will cherish you and love you

with love,

your Heart

12. Building

Keep building

you are onto something

keep building

you are an emerging spirit

keep building

you have your sacred mission to attain

sink your gaze

into golden rivers

wrap your heart

around liquid crystals

feel the fire from within

the fire that burns cold

and drives all that lives

look within

and be a channel

of all the wonders

let them flow through you

you are ready

open up

open up without fear

with calmness, fervor and a heart

let them come to you

from faraway in the expanse

and closer into your dreams

let them talk through you

becoming them,

embrace those words

and share them

for all to bathe

in light, in love, in truth

let your life flow

and miracles

will follow

13. A channel

I let liquid light run through me

liquid light that hugs me

from within

when I let it flow

I remember

all

I know

all

I hear

all

I sense

all

I am

all

beyond what the world offers

to our touch, or smell, or sight, or ear

beyond all that

lives a world

far removed

yet within

the real world

just seemingly outside our reach

the moment we surrender

it comes, rushing

from within

bright, innate, alive, everlasting

closer than a millimeter

hiding right inside of time

awaiting us to sense it

eager to come and play with us

for us to notice

impatient to guide us into our dreams

we all are living

into a shared dream

living in an Eden

with abundance, joy and laughter

little do we know

it is hidden right in plain sight

awaiting us to look inside

right here - right now

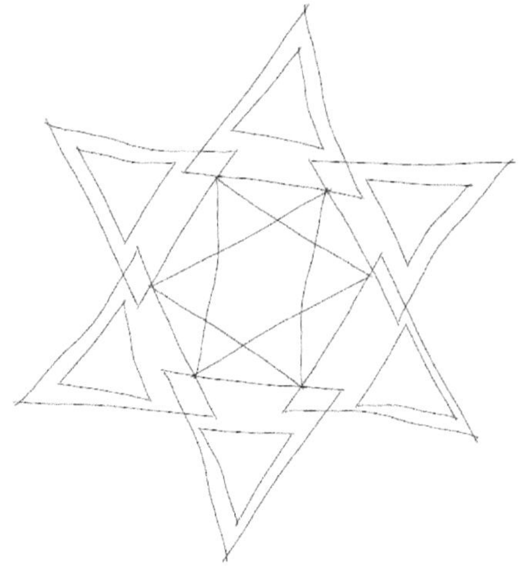

14. Birds

I see sparkles

in your eyes

when I look inside

I lay my being in your palm

quietly and gently

I am tiny birds feeding from your hand

happy, chirping

playfully fluttering their wings

they trust you

they feel your warmth

they are a piece of nature

entrusting their life to you

I am the sunshine on your face

gently stroking your cheeks and smile

you are deeply gentle

caring

your heart

cherishes connection

your soul

thirsty for

the love you crave

be gentle with the tiny birds

let the sun shine on your sides

for if you shun them

they will scatter

leave you all alone

if you scare them,

they will fly away

and who knows

if they will find it in themselves

to come back

15. Anne

Little lady

dressed in a long, rough

gray ragged dress

you did nothing wrong

it was a mob

a mob,

armed with

the most dangerous of weapons

fear.

stones.

you scared them to death

you threatened their simple lives

they had all

told themselves

that they're simple, poor, and hungry

you dared to question it

for yourself

but they took it

personally

they saw in you

a threat

to their imagined poor, hungry lives

if you are right, then they are wrong

and they lived

as victims

of circumstance, the king, and nature

all in vain

they wasted

their own lives

if you are right, and they are wrong

they lived a lie -

a lie they made up

of fear, of habit

unreal.

victims of their own hand

lives ended

before they began to live

your pure heart

seemed like a life sentence

to the mob

don't fear them, child.

love them.

they didn't know

they will see it, too

on the day that they depart

and then they will be compelled

by their truest heart of hearts

to come back

and learn

the precious lesson

that we all

learn.

we are love

made of love, forever, deeply

many worlds away

and yet within,

there is a single heart

that beams us timeless love

and one day

we all

will see it with our truest heart of hearts

and until then, child,

don't fret

you did nothing wrong

there's nothing to understand

there's nothing to undo

there's nothing you mischieved

there's nothing right or wrong

your pure heart

simply scared them to death

your own

rebirth

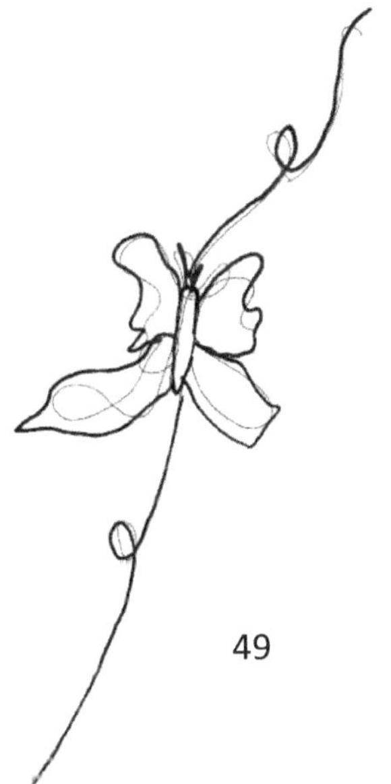

16. Agraba

Little boy

on the streets

of Agraba

underfed

clothed in rags

confused

dirty

hungry

and alone

alone, in the whole Creation

little boy,

you are not alone!

the world is not against you

wash off your sobs

quieten your sorrows

clean up your anger

soothe your tears

you are precious

a dear droplet of god

smile

let your heart fly

with joy

and play

you are just about five –

rejoice!

you are an internal

fire

deep within

the colour of a lightning

forgive them

love them

they all, truly, did their best

they gave you

the best shot they

possibly could

the best shot

they knew how

you are loved

you are beautiful

you are whole

now rest. and love.

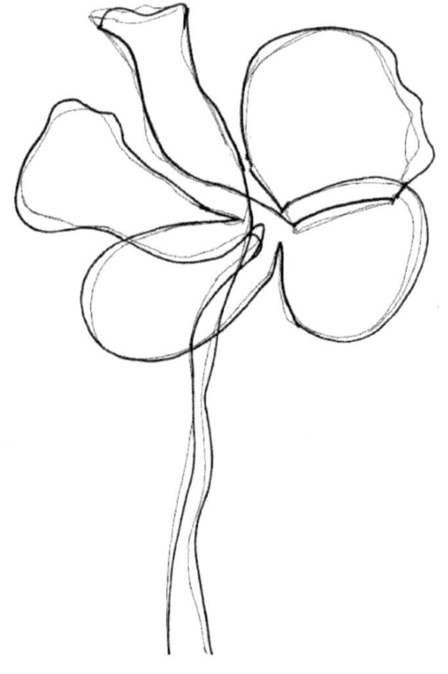

17. The ashes of Pompeii

…are my ashes

a cloud so thick

so heavy

black

came onto me

that's all

the end

of a simple life

on cobble-stone streets

my friends, my love

staring at it

like a statue

a statue made of flesh

my heart was racing

my feet glued to the stone

my dress the grey of ashes – so I
thought

those ashes bore another god

an angry god

wrath

who am I to try to run away?

as if I could

outrun

the will of god

I didn't try

I was but a girl

fresh with hopes

to marry neighbour's merry lad

I was but a youth

still unspoilt by life

that angry god

was after me

but why?

my heart was running

yet at a standstill

that's how I met her

death

with opened eyes

and racing heart

as if made of stone myself

as I was meant to be

swallowed whole by an angry god

for sins I had not yet accomplished

in my own-made gray dress

there, in the middle of the street

halfway home, halfway out

suffocating

then... nothing

silence

loud silence

stillness

the chatter stopped.

the bustling of the street

the women screaming

all that's left is I

and an angry god

with ash of fire, the colour of charcoal

deeper grey than grey –

the colour wrath

and wrath from hereby,

not above and not below

but why?

it's even darker now

and awfully quite

peacefully quite. tranquil even.

just darkness, in and out

all around

and within

where's me?

18. Sound

It speaks to my heart
the resonance grabs and shakes me
in the gentlest way

like a sieve full of flower
when it's held just right
all that does not belong
seeps underneath

is freed

my body is a sieve
and emotions are that fine dust
the sound reverberates

through me

and leaves inside only what belongs
all the worries simply seep away

love remains

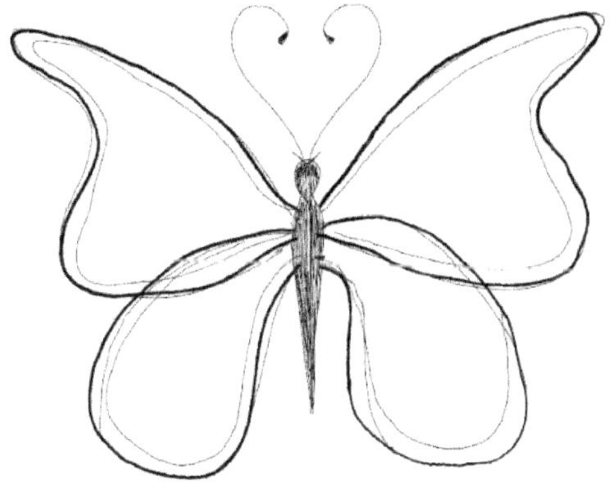

19. Morning

I stepped outside

of time

and witnessed

the universe

naked

stripped of forms and limits

beautiful

breath-taking

there I don't breathe

I just am but who is me?

liquid crystals

bright and flowing

are my companions

and flowers

flowers made of gold

alive

swirling, raining out within that expanse

are my companions

golden breathing lines

and ripples

spirals

they have come to greet me

we are one

connected

where am I?

20. In the end

Once upon a time

it felt like a broken heart

as if

they took it

as if

they smashed it

as if

it shattered

I learned its secret:

I am a ball of light

and my heart

kccpc within

a power so primal

a power so pervasive

that no piece of matter, harshness, hatred

could make the tiniest a scratch!

I know now

that all comes from within:

the light, the love, the life.

and my heart is always open

it is a luscious gift

my heart is my source

unending, limitless, and everlasting

without a beginning

and without end.

67